Jane Campbell

To Patrick
Thanx for all the
years of help in the
writers group
Mav

Slowly as Clouds

indigo dreams poetry

Indigo Dreams Publishing

First Edition: Slowly as Clouds
First published in Great Britain in 2022 by:
Indigo Dreams Publishing
24, Forest Houses
Cookworthy Moor
Halwill
Beaworthy
Devon
EX21 5UU

www.indigodreamspublishing.com

ISBN 978-1-912876-68-6

British Library Cataloguing in Publication Data. A CIP record for this book can be obtained from the British Library.

Designed and typeset in Palatino Linotype by Indigo Dreams.
Cover photograph by Gareth Parry : Author photo Kitchou Bry.
Cover design by Ronnie Goodyer at Indigo Dreams.
Printed and bound in Great Britain by 4edge Ltd.

Papers used by Indigo Dreams are recyclable products made from wood grown in sustainable forests following the guidance of the Forest Stewardship Council.

To my family of friends
who have loved and supported me all my life.

ACKNOWLEDGEMENTS

Thank you...
...to my darling Red, as you know I couldn't have done without you and wouldn't ever want to.
...to Helen May Williams, for interrogating my verbs, winkling out lacunae and being my Ezra Pound.
...to the Poetry Matters Collective, the West Wales Stanza group and Lampeter Writers who were honest, kind, generous and always there.

Acknowledgement of first publication are:
Beltane was included in The Rapture edition of Black Bough 2021.
Mighty in One Hand Clapping, 2020.
Last Dance in The Dawntreader winter edition 2021/2022.
Degrading was published under the title *Beneath* in Bloody Amazing Anthology by Dragon Yaffle.
Compost Loo was in Swansea Poetry Slam Anthology 2021.
The City Park won the Void Poetry contest in AsianCha Magazine 2014.
Wishing Well in Well, Dam (Beautiful Dragons Collective).
The Gardener was performed on BBC Radio Wales, 'Giants in the Sky' programme.

CONTENTS

Slowly as Clouds

Beltane

her breath
earthy as
wild hyacinth
deep in the glade

we roll on green and purple blue
crinkled in crone skin
her fingers beat time inside my heart

slowly as clouds
May moaning from our mouths

Mighty

I dreaded us losing
our Gruffalo dad
an army of hands and feet
the strict skin of him towering
so hard to kiss

Now softened to this heap in a hospital bed
he lets me warm-oil-massage
his giant hands
pleads
sing me to sleep
slowly

The Ways

Beyond the measure found in worn threads
on our treasured bed, I love your soft smile
fragile folds of crows-feet, the slowing walk.

Watching your rocking gait, I appreciate
the days we danced filled with moon,
pushed each other over into clover.

Perhaps if we had never-ending lives
I'd have made us wait: left you for later
and never known *this,* us-entwined.

Because all knots must one day be undone,
I'm thrilled my time on earth is fixed. My hand
was forced to make sure it was you I kissed.

Heavenbound

I want to die singing, swinging from
a sex-sling strung up in a seedy club.
Won't groan while I go, I'll moan coming.
Spoon the moon in a smirk of mauve
to the cheers of a crowd I will
force my heartbeat far too far till
she pops like a cherry just when I'm
ready to go all the way homeward.

Not available in shops or stores
with a DIY death, the choice stays yours.

Relation-ship

The first rains
washed away our clothes
left deep wrinkles
fully exposed.
Naked we began to navigate
test our ship shapes till
we gained together-pull.
Hauled and heaved
set open all our secret sails,
started to believe in diligent caulking
and tacked towards
warm safe shores;
my lips downy hair
kissing yours.

Let go

The only thing we both know
is that we can't let go.

Once, we were the only show
we wanted to watch:
now we're a stale rerun,
knots that have been undone
longer than either of us want to believe.

All of love is opportunity,
even when the sheets are clean
never to get dirty again.
All of this linen
we keep trying to wash is
stained indelibly with us.

If I don't want to be lovers
It doesn't mean
I don't still love us.

Last Dance

One long-feared moment now to explore
when death beckons you to the dance floor.

You peel back the blankets from that bed
trip bare feet to the garden instead.

Open to the storm's wild crescendo,
let rain spin your skin to her tempo.

Slide-step in the ecstasy of joy
laugh at escape plans you tried to deploy.

Then lie down quilted by leaf shadow
as night birds lullaby your way home.

Your people will find you in time,
garlanded in dawn's dewdrop rime.

Nineteen Eighty-Five

Whatever happened
to sleek long-distance swimmer
gentleman Jon?
Something shuffled in his tarot pack:
the hanged man
suspended upside down
fell out with his rent-boy housemates
all in the acquired-immune-deficient state.

Jon at nineteen had been sanguine
in the spat-on face of death.
Suddenly though he snapped in
like a frenzied dancing fan,
furious that his pact with the bad-news devil
hadn't cured him.

Jon went wild coyote
spitting shit,
lurked in bars for prey to infect,
but those cheap tricks smelt like
a bitter cock-pit
then days and nights alone in the dark,
facing the wall
under a duvet of drugs and drink,
pausing only in the loo
to flush his sick spunk down.

Jon, once spirit dancer, sea-otter man,
now out of reach to our rafting hands.

Metamorphosis

Can we afford all this?
Dad asks as I cast fairy lights around his hospital bed.
I sellotape big photos of our loved ones to the wall,
turn Christy Moore on the tape player next to a stack of books.
He believes he is in an expensive hotel room.
His next question is not so sweet
Will it be messy?
I know he fears indignity at the very end.
I stick up pictures of butterflies
We talk of cocoons and the way his pupa state
will melt into mush before his wings can grow.

I sleep every night on the chair beside him:
there to fetch the nurse for pain relief.
Recently though he has spurned this.
It might be his one and only death, he doesn't want to miss it.
Taking ages though isn't it?

The urgency not to miss this grand finale
builds in me too.
He'll go when it's his time,
nod other family members, there to whisper his favourite poetry
or pop in on their way home from school to say goodbye.
Ireland really is a great place to die.

Then after two bunkered weeks
Nurse Orla tells me she can siphon his fluid-filled lungs
a few more times.
Make this the last time
I blurt. After two weeks' grotty sleep I'm raving,
scared I will see him die in panic, flail drowning.

I recite the creatures he will evolve into
You'll be butterfly, then rabbit,
then antelope
I hear myself be a chattering child.
I stiffen as his tendons pull tight,
wide eyes already without sight.
Then he just dies.
No mess no horror
only release.

His face relaxes into youthful peace.

Differently

If I were a time-traveller and
could redo the dodgy days
that first moment I met you
I'd kiss you right away

if I were a lot younger
I'd cycle to Nepal
lie about on warm beaches,
build fires, play volley-ball

but nobody's immortal
I've twenty-summers left I'd say
to recognise the silver lining
hidden in cloud today

We love inside the story of loss

I can't believe that I, like you,
will come to an ordinary end,
breathing out then
never in again.

This fevered buzz on a ball,
fungal blooms who eat decay,
popcorn bursting inside the microwave of time,
despite the fact our sun too will die one day.

How can we dance at this party
now that we can count the cost.
How do we love inside
the story of loss?

My Present

(for Aylan Shenu: refugee child
drowned on TV at three years old.)

I wrap this body
in the finest tabloid paper:
tie quality strings
with tight little knots.

What else can I do with
my celebrated son
but send him to your better world
filled with food, shelter and toys.

I whisper a last goodbye
as I place him on a postal scale,
weighing him heavy against
the price of hope.

But we both know
he'll grow cold this Christmas
under plastic needle trees
with their fake magic dreams.

Go Gently

Asleep she is curled,
the tip of a fern
in embryonic roll.
Soft spine undulates
prepares to return her
to her ancient form.

Birth spurted her
from her mother's womb
onto bombed Birmingham earth.
to organise a strike,
call for a living wage,
appear on television,
impress her daughter
with the importance of rights,
that once they had bite,
were revoked.

Title makes reference to *Do Not Go Gently Into That Good Night* by Dylan Thomas, 1947.

Mum

You love her now
her dragon suit is torn,
claws pared,
scorch doused down.

You love her toothless
nappied, needy, compliant
child for you to dandle,
feed and nurse.

But don't forget her
rages, derailed desires.
Once upon a time
she savaged you with fire.

Rest in Peace

As the cat settles for a cosy nap,
my chest inflames and infected pain
forces through a warning wheeze.
I hear death's first siren chant.

To my mum who lies dying,
I send this incantation,
Forget your fear of lightning,
the broken glass is all cleared away.
Go gently sister-mother.

We never made it to friends
with patriarchy doing his usual number.
Baby from between your legs: not daughter
but site-specific dangerous reminder.

Evergreen

I kiss the poisonous yew
because I love her anyway,
green redeemer from winter grey,
bold evergreen resilient who

feeds from even feeble light,
survives by being dangerous prey
when leafless skeleton trees play dead
their summer sugars stored away.

Inspired, I expose myself whole,
spurn the easy shedding way,
keep a little venom in my veins
as antidote to life's decay.

Fairy tale

I shouldn't have
tortured you Mumma
for the scary tales
you told me
where every little
girl gets got.

It wasn't you
that made the wolves,
rammed us into
those rape plots,
but I got shocked,
lashed out and
the messenger
got shot.

Mum and her Da

Sheila says she's just in love with her Da,
won't come out of that dream for nobody.
Her Mum's got a GI so she don't care.
They're just a freaky kind of family
and Romeo and Juliet were teens
in the greatest romance that's ever been.
Daring yes, beyond classical to myth.
My mum tells me that I need to know this:
they both enjoyed sexual bliss, she
too beautiful for any man to resist.
Then he invited round her Uncle Bill.
My mum left in the clothes she stood up in,
never forgave her own stupidity.

It was the oldest story ever told
how men turn to children as wives grow old.

Entanglement

I have in my bag a crammed house.
It spills stuff onto other people's settees,
forces me to secretly shy-rinse
around strangers' taps,
wipe mirrors and
put away their dirty pants.

After Mum's divorce, home shrunk to a spiral
inside a curled seashell. She trawled car boot sales
busy with ceramic frogs and knick-knackery.
Slowly she hid us under her treasure blanket.
I did not dare to turn around too quickly
in case the chaos collapsed.

Cobwebs began to festoon the stacks,
spooled loops from door-tops to picture frames.
Cinderella became my full-time job.
My childish bare feet made paths over mouldy paperwork.
Resentful I dusted a jostle of trinkets
hoovered the aisles of trustworthy things.

Today I stand on a threshold
when you, my new love, ask for help
to sort your room bulging with littered sadness.
Despite the time passed
in the heft of my bag I discover
I'm still too angry for drudgery.

Tread gently

Sunday evenings
after all afternoon baking
in the radio four warmed kitchen
while Mum slept slumped
exhausted in front of the TV
I would parachute in
soft as a dandelion,
try to wake her gently
avoid the usual chagrin.
But as usual she came to,
all bitter spittle,
demanding what are you doing?
Despite my pains
I had failed again in my quest
to wake her beautifully.

I would never know
all those years I lived at home,
that it was her Dad
who made her wake up so.

Love's Recovery

Then after a lifetime
I walk into your final bedroom,
to find you happy
fizzy in your chest
at news of my success.
Somehow we've passed
through the narrowest place.

You ask if you were a *ghastly mum*
but after all we've been through
I gift you a gentle lie
that you were kind and easy to love
and in this moment
it is truer than true.

Warrior

Thumb-sized fledgling wren
taking her first flight,
all crimson-lined beckoning beak,

gazes gormless
from our hawthorn hedge,
till a sudden maternal streak

shrieks interference
to scare off
the bear in me.

Dog Fox...

saunters through sheep.
They chew ryegrass
as if he smells like green
or fresh-born lamb.

I think of sneak-thief pocket-picking,
of so many blind eyes turning.
When will we learn
a sixth sense queasy with lies?

Veracity is an acquired taste.
You'd think that we'd have one by now:
a way to pick fake,
males on the make.

We negotiate perpetual youth:
(you look lovely in that shirt).
What if we could cud
What if we would ruminate?

Winter Solstice

Retreated into a midwinter moment
any being that can, sleeps.
Distant rumbles of cattle or clouds
rub together as calm lengthens to miles.
Room now for every molecule to breathe.
I stroll my cold feet through this tranquillity,
wear two dressing gowns,
clutch a hot cup of tea.
My ears grope for sound,
for worm wiggle or snore of bee,
but nothing stirs
or is disturbed by me.

Degrading

Angry older girls,
rulers of St Mary's school
mob me in a cubicle,
pressure me for proof
of playground claims
that my first period
despite my youth
has already come.
My pants are dragged down
as I'm forced centre of a sorry stage;
recasting them
in perpetuity
slow for their age.

Playing Cemetery

When I was a child I played long days
in my local cemetery, vast space
impressive and gory, where I tried on
adult-sized emotions for the deaths of
children—*far too terribly young.*
One day, twilight-skipping home, I saw that
my street led directly to this dead end.
Parents dismissed my mawkish questions,
just part of life dear, but Dad waited
for me to see his legacy, peaceful
death in the flesh, leaving me to advent
calendar my remaining days; grateful.

Death anchors me through my course of heartbeats
or else I'd drift, day-dream my whole life's time.

Handmade home

Pulling leaves from my gutter
inside a sleepy sunshine,

once I had a whole house to build
before winter should storm in.

I calmed my mind
with fantasies of restful futures,

when there would only be a bit of
low-ladder muck to clear away,

and suddenly I am here,
now today.

Cake

at fifty
to be finally
sitting beside a fire
kindled from trees I planted as seeds
tended…watered…slept curled beneath
on hot summer days until...they were ready to be
coppice cut…on this clear January…big birthday
with friends singing…brought bundled home
dry store seasoned…then chopped and
burned while we were all eating
home grown carrot soup.
That is cake.

Planet of the Cats

Earth erosion exposes
ancient artefacts.
Life so different before
our species was
in charge.

As ice-melt removes a veil
we gaze in awe at the
habitat of house-sized cats,
undeniable bones
hardened into fossil rock,
claws caught like scythes in trees,
dog-sized fleas,
floors beaten flat by elephantine paws
and tiny humans,
kept as pets.

Hunger

Alone in a landscape
of white fondant icing, I am
squeezed into that strait-jacket dress and those high heels.
My red velvet stilettos sink in beneath
the soft sugar surface
to plough up pink buttercream.

Suddenly the cloying smells break me
vanilla, chocolate, raspberry and marzipan.
I hurl my body down, face-deep in sweet sponge furrow.
My bin-bag belly drags the floor
as I begin to creep feed,
forcing great gobs of gateau into
my far too tiny mouth.

Twenty-twenty vision

Marie slowly strolls home from the garden,
day spent bent in the leafy green tunnel.
Like everyone she can't know what's to come.
When nightmare zombies stalk her closed eyes,
she refuses by habit to be undone:
forces fears to spark up a blaze of busyness,
forks over her stinkiest compost beds,
uses sleepless nights to sort out the slugs,
and frantically repairs that old woodshed.
When joy finds her, floured fingers baking:
she's thankful for the path she has taken.

Exchanging cakes for apples Marie remembers,
she's only as full as the belly of her neighbours.

Compost Loo

We built a room with a millionaire's view
to do in nature what animals do,
to bury ourselves one shit at a time.
We sit on a wooden throne made by hand
return what was borrowed from the land,
waste into fertiliser for absolutely free
safely deposit it far from the sea,
so mother Earth is enriched
passing through us,
as we go passing through.

Mortality saves me

Nature gently hints
the coming of my going
in tints of grey hairs,
four eyes, less teeth
petty losses that loose my grip,
slack off the pleasure
of hard toffees,
exhausting travel trips.

Soon I will climb
on the funicular bus.
My last request of death
to ginger-up
every sunlit sea sparkle,
drive me not to die with
legs that could have walked further,
trance-danced harder.

Christmas swim!

Christmas swim! other people cry,
with leaves torn from trees
and icebergs floating by?
but the splat patter
of my over-exposed feet
willingly toe the frigid shallows
before I plunge legs, liver and face
below pale jade waves.

Mind has wanted all its life
to join the daring-do
but my body signals panic shallow breath
as cold-burn overwhelms me.
Then suddenly I'm numb
to everything but seagull song,
salt tang on my lips and
I'm really doing this.

I turn to head for shore
absolutely nothing left
except the one gift
worth having
beating gloriously in my chest.

Always Alice

At 600 years-old deep in her comfy sofa,
camera held high for a slimmer selfie,
Alice shows off her latest face in
funky death-denial drag.

Her four metres squared is empty,
six walls all screens interactive
the world waits baited to watch her show
but Alice feels sexually unattractive.

Stem cells regrow damaged body-parts,
Alice can drink till her liver's done in
using tv, pills or tragedy to take her away,
she is still stuck fast in now.

Alice longs for lovers whose desires survive
the relentless sunrises of always alive.
Immortality has rotted
any freshness away.

Candy crush could only take her so far.
In a life without end,
minutes became millennia
time turned jailer from friend.

Fierce Felines

What cruel cats we'd be
however clever
with no dependable death
if life
was only
forever.

Power

At winter crisis
with no sun
        a lean-seed dreams
of full summer fun.

To Do

1. find the cat a new lap
2. drag bed outside (mosquito net)
3. explain to the family #gently
4. lay my treasure out on the garden wall
5. dance till the whole sun comes up
6. b r e a t h e
7. kiss you my lovers
8. sip slowly on that poppy tea.

Fear Lies Beneath

Below us lives Dragon,
so fetid
his breath
chokes our dreams
with acrid smoke.

Each day our sun
evaporates the grim traces
and then we can pretend
our monster
stays slayed.

The City Park

Is held in a hug of filthy plane trees
bred for the burden
of inhaling London smokes.

By dawn a team of trench-coated crows
solemn as a forensic squad stalk the
new-mown grass for discarded body parts,

ignore black clad joggers
huff-puffing with invisible friends
who scuff dusty paths parallel to the municipal track,

who pass the shifty dog-shit sitters
urgently rustling plastic bags
anxious to cue their charges to produce in a convenient space.

Chaotic mist barely clings to our aviator sky.
While Gaia with her wired-up toothless jaw,
like the London trees, is dry.

Rebellion

Once upon a time
we lived on the perfect planet,
not too hot, not too cold.

Now begonia blooms,
blousy and tough as forever,
lie broken by remorseless storms.

As the hungry clock grinds away,
we pray Gaia has a plan
to save these bare skins

but we must also bolt
our soft animal bodies under cars
to resist the drive towards extinction.

Wishing Well

"Village women visited me,
tucked long skirts up against mudding,
leaned in deep to suckle my flow.
Like lovers we face-gazed;
sometimes the only mirror they would know.
I listened to every mother's tale,
played favourites in the public spats,
then cooled ankles to reduce swell,
befriended their bags of thirst
as they banked on me,
demanded I determine destinies.
Not enough
to dissolve mountains,
lubricate land,
they brought me a poor runty babe,
or stumbled heavy down my earth steps
draped with an ailing parent
they could not afford to care for.

Local legend lore still believes
a night on my slate bed-slab
will conjure kill or cure,
but I dread the cries of guttering despair
when wishes are whispered once again
into votive ribbons
tied into my hawthorn hair."

Ffynonn-wen: St Cybi's well in Llangybi, Ceredigion,
said to cure scurvy and rheumatism

The Gardener

When I die please bury me
in this orchard full of fruit trees.
Plant me like the cherries,
apples and plums I grew.
Don't box me up but lower my limbs naked
in an earthy shroud down in the rich brown soil.
Watch me bloom in the dark
towards a million wormy mouths who
recast every fold into a feast for fungi.
Let Gaia's grains absorb me back to her stores.
My body yearns to be compost,
free again to drink clouds from spring rain,
to be bark, branches, buds, leaves,
part of plum, cherry and apple too,
for I shall be the garden then
and the gardener will be you.

Indigo Dreams Publishing Ltd
24, Forest Houses
Cookworthy Moor
Halwill
Beaworthy
Devon
EX21 5UU
www.indigodreamspublishing.com